EILEEN GADEN

BREADS

MANNA FROM HEAVEN

Christian Herald Books
40 Overlook Drive, Chappaqua, New York 10514

MANNA FROM ḣEAVEN

And there was no bread in all the land; for the famine was very sore, so that the land of Egypt and all the land of Canaan fainted by reason of the famine.

GENESIS 47:13

People of Israel were accustomed to hard times. Not always was the Holy Land the "land of milk and honey." In Egypt famine occured if there was any change in the rainfall and the proper overflow of the Nile. The most devastating famine recorded in the Bible was in the time of Joseph, who forecast the coming catastrophe by interpreting Pharaoh's dream of "seven empty ears blasted with the east wind" to mean there would be seven years of famine (Genesis 41:27). Other problems plagued the children of Israel in Egypt when the same "east wind brought the locust . . . they covered the face of the whole earth . . . and they did eat every herb of the land and all the fruit of the trees" (Exodus 10:13, 15).

Before they reached Canaan and were wandering in the desert, their hunger was severe. And God miraculously provided food: "And the children of Israel did eat manna for forty years, until they came to a land inhabited" (Exodus 16:35). Manna was probably an excretion from minute insects that ate the leaves of the tamarisk trees. It could be gathered each day after the dew had gone and before it was melted by the sun (Exodus 16:14, 15, 21). If it had not been for this

BREADS MANNA FROM HEAVEN

"bread of heaven," they indeed might have perished.

But there were good years when the fields brought forth abundant crops of grain. Wheat and barley were the most important grains grown throughout the Holy Land, and they have flourished in Egypt and Palestine ("a land of wheat and barley" Deuteronomy 8:8) since the dawn of time. In the Old Testament days, barley was more widespread than wheat, because it could grow in poorer soil and survive heat and drought better than any other grain. It was the universal food of the peasant and was considered a symbol of poverty and humility. King Solomon seems to have taken advantage of its rich abundance, since the laborers who built his lavish temple required a daily ration of more than twenty thousand measures of barley!

In Egypt and Palestine some wheat was trodden by oxen and pressed upon the ground by a cart wheel, just as described in Isaiah 28:28. Barley and other grains were threshed and winnowed by the farmer, and were usually ground into meal and flour by the women of the family, whose long day began before dawn when they heated the first fire for the daily work of continuous baking.

First, grain kernels from lentils, millet, barley or wheat had to be ground, usually with a kind of mortar and pestle approach, using a "rubbing stone" or a heavy handmill. The rubbing stone was really made of two slabs—one shaped almost like a saddle and often more than two and one-half feet long, and the second, a thinner, convex rock between which the grains were crushed. A handmill could also be employed in grinding. Here the upper stone had a wooden handle in the shape of a peg, which was worn smooth and had a hole in the center through which the grain was poured. This upper stone was rotated in a full circle by the handle, crushing the grain on a second stone beneath it. So important was the handmill to the survival of a family, that in the Book of Deuteronomy a creditor is forbidden from accepting a household's millstone as a pledge, because in doing so "he taketh a man's life in pledge" (Deuteronomy 24:6).

A fairly smooth-textured meal resulted from all this strenuous grinding. To produce "fine flour" favored by the palates of the rich or for sacred breads, this meal would be re-ground several times, or sifted through sieves until it resembled the packaged kind we buy today.

Sometimes the wheat was not baked into bread, but boiled without being ground to make a thick kind of porridge, known as "burghul." Kernels of wheat and barley just harvested might be roasted on an iron plate or in a pan, thus becoming parched corn. These crisp kernels were carried in the pockets of the nomads on their long treks into the desert or eaten with bread as part of the everyday meal.

Abraham gives the first bread recipe in the Bible when he tells his wife Sarah to bake "a morsel of bread" (Genesis 18:5) for the three angels of the Lord who visit him: "And Abraham hastened into the tent unto Sarah, and said, 'Make ready quickly three measures of fine meal, knead it, and make cakes upon the hearth' " (Genesis 18:6).

In Old Testament times, breadmaking was well established as a profession, and the Hebrews probably learned the basics of this culinary art from the Egyptians. Found on the tomb of Rameses II (he was probably the pharaoh whose oppression led to the Exodus) is an interesting story in pictures of an Egyptian bakery and confectionary. On one side are two men leaning on staffs and kneading dough with their feet. In the center, a baker is stamping out animal and geometrically shaped dough for the fancy cakes. In another area, a pastry cook holds a spiral-shaped cake which he had just baked in an oven, much like our barbecue grill with a lid covering the wood fire.

For the simpler Hebrews, however, the ordinary loaf of bread was round with a diameter from five to sixteen inches. Some were "as thick as a finger;" others were thin as paper. For offerings, the bread was often cooked in pans.

Shewbreads were sacred and used only as an offering in the temple in the Old Testament. "Shewbread" or "showbread" or "the bread of the Presence" consisted of twelve loaves of unleavened bread which were always found on a long wooden table in the holy part of the temple open only to its priests. A symbol of God's abundance and grace, each week a fresh supply of this holy offering was baked and placed in the inner sanctum. It was this shewbread which the hungry David persuaded the keepers of the temple to feed him and his soldiers: "So the priest gave him hallowed bread, for there was no bread there but the shewbread, that was taken from before the Lord" (I Samuel 21:6). Later when the Pharisees accuse Christ and his disciples of eating food unlawfully and working on the Sabbath, Christ tells the story of David's taking of the holy offering: "Have ye not read, what David did, when he was an hungered . . . How he entered into the house of God, and did eat the shewbread" (Matthew 12:3, 4).

Unleavened bread was made by mixing flour, salt, and water in a wooden basin or "kneading trough." This dough was then molded by hand into flat discs and baked. These unleavened cakes were called "matstah" or "mazzah." It was just such bread which the Hebrews cooked in haste on the night of their escape with Moses:

> *And they baked unleavened cakes of the dough which they brought forth out of Egypt, for it was not leavened; because they were thrust out of Egypt, and could not tarry.*
>
> *Exodus 12:39*

Even today, during the eight days of Passover which commemorate the Hebrew's escape from bondage and the coming of the spring harvest, no bread or other leavened baked foods may be eaten in homes where this holiday is celebrated.

Usually, however, bread was allowed to rise, and a small lump of "starter dough" from the last day's baking was added to the new batch. The mixture was then set aside and allowed to ferment. Biblical cooks even had the equivalent of our commercial baking powder, which is made of soda, cream of tartar, flour and corn starch. Soda was obtained from the ashes of plants, and tartar from the crude substance found adhering to the sides of wine casks. The tartar was ground up, dissolved in boiling water and then filtered through charcoal. For a thickening agent which resembled our cornstarch, wheat starch was used. This was refined from three month wheat which was very light in weight.

As flavoring agents for their cakes and sweets, biblical people had a choice of ground almond, pungent grasses, seeds, herbs and fruit syrup flavored with spices. Sometimes the dough was mixed with olive oil and cumin seeds, with honey, cinnamon or saffron to add a little extra flavor and color.

Once the dough had risen, whatever its ingredients, there were three different ways to fire the bread. The "cake baked on the coals" for the prophet Elijah (I Kings 19:6) was prepared by the first and oldest method. First a few flat stones were gathered together and a fire was built upon them. After the stones were red-hot, the embers were raked off, the bread was laid on the stones and covered over with embers and ashes. After a while the ashes were removed and the cake was baked on the other side. When the demanding prophet Hosea rebuked the people of Israel for their wickedness, he used this baking style to describe the Israelite's leader: "Ephraim, he hath mixed himself among the people; Ephraim is a cake not turned" (Hosea: 7:8). And so, the next time someone comes up with a "half-baked" idea, you'll know the phrase comes piping hot from the pages of the Old Testament!

Bread was also prepared in another way, by placing a curved, bowl-like iron plate directly over a small fire built into the ground or in a small fireplace at the corner of a family tent. The uncooked bread was then placed on the metal and fired into steaming cakes. Even today the nomads of the Holy Land carry this portable "hot plate" or pan with them on their journeys through the desert.

Once the people of Bible times had settled down to become farmers and artisans, they used an oven called a "tannur" for their baking. In one type, heated stones were piled up and a large clay bowl oven was placed over them. Heat was applied from the outside and bread was baked on the stones within. A larger cone-shaped jar oven, and later a pit oven were also used for baking. Here the oven was heated by burning shrubs, twigs, dried roots, and animal dung, which were placed at the bottom of the oven. As the fuel burned, the cake dough was slapped onto the inside walls of the oven where it was quickly baked by the intense heat.

It was this last oven which was used by the professional bakers who flourished in those times. The services of these men were in such demand that there was a street in Jerusalem especially set off for their special trade. When the prophet Jeremiah was given royal protection, the king Zedekiah commanded that he should be given "daily a piece of bread from out of the bakers' street, until all the bread in the city were spent" (Jeremiah 37:21).

The bakers who once marketed their goods in old Jerusalem prepared a wide range of "bake meats" as described in the Old Testament—from the pancake loaf and flat barley cake to thin, waferlike disks of bread coated with honey or oil. For lighter confectionary treats, they whipped their dough and added eggs to their batter, often sweetening it with raisins and honey or flavoring it with pistachio and almond oils and nutmeats.

During the time when Christians began to worship openly in Rome, a dough was made consisting of flour, salt, and water. Bakers fashioned the dough into thin rolls, formed each into two arms crossed in prayer to remind them that Lent was a season of penance and prayer. They were called *bracalle,* the Latin word meaning "little arms." Many years later the Germans referred to them as *brezel.* They are known to us today as pretzels.

Bread was closely associated with Christ, not only because of his miracle of feeding the masses with five barley loaves (John 6:9), but from his birth. He was born in Bethlehem, which means "house of bread." Apparently, its name came from its location in the center of a productive grain area. Whether baked at home or brought fresh from the market place, bread was never cut, but always broken by hand. Christ often "breaks bread" with his disciples. Hot, savory bread rounds were served in light wicker baskets and morsels of the bread were given by the head of the household to the rest of the family and to guests. Bits of the broken bread were used almost like spoons to scoop out the hot food at mealtime. Most often this hot food was eaten from the communal bowl made of earthenware, wood, leather or copper. The Last Supper shared by Christ and his apostles began in just this way:

> *And as they did eat, Jesus took bread, and blessed, and brake it, and gave to them . . .*
>
> *Mark 14:22*

MAKING YEAST BREADS

YEAST

One package of active dry granular yeast is equal to a scant tablespoon.

Compressed or fresh yeast is available in 0.6, 1 and 2 ounce cakes. Keep in refrigerator or freezer; defrost to room temperature and use as soon as possible. Compressed yeast and active dry yeast can be used interchangeably.

FLOUR

For the recipes in this book the flour need not be sifted. When measuring fill the measure to overflowing and level off with a spatula. Do not shake or tap before leveling. Flour made in a blender from barley, whole wheat, millet and other grains will vary in coarseness and the liquid added may have to be adjusted.

LIQUIDS

All liquids must be used at correct temperatures—105°F. to 115°F. If no thermometer is available, the liquid should feel comfortably warm when a few drops are put on the inside of the wrist. If liquid is too hot the bread will not rise, if too cold the bread will rise too slowly.

BEATING

Beat the first amount of flour, yeast and liquid for about 2 minutes. For batter breads beat until batter leaves side of bowl.

KNEADING

Lightly flour hands and work surface. Turn dough onto surface and shape into a ball. Pull up edge of dough farthest from you and fold it over the top surface. Using the heels of your hands push the dough away with a rolling motion. Turn dough one quarter around and repeat rolling and turning until the dough is smooth and elastic, about 8 to 10 minutes. If dough sticks, flour hands and surface again. Place ball of kneaded dough in a greased bowl and turn it over to grease top. Cover bowl with a clean cloth and let rise in a warm place until double in bulk.

RISING

Dough, except refrigerator-type doughs, will rise best in a warm place (80 to 85°F.) which can be obtained by any one of the following methods: (a) place a covered bowl of dough in unheated oven with a large pan filled with hot water beneath it (b) place covered bowl of dough on a wire rack over a pan of hot water (c) place covered bowl of dough in a deep pan of warm water, not hot. First rising takes from 1 to 1 1/2 hours.

TESTING

To test dough for "double in bulk" press tips of two fingers lightly 1/2 inch into the dough. If dent remains dough is ready to punch down.

PUNCHING DOWN

Push fist into the center of the dough. Gather the edges of the dough to the center and turn the dough over.

SHAPING LOAVES

Lightly flour rolling pin and roll dough into a 8 by 12 inch rectangle. Starting with the 8 inch end, tightly roll dough towards you. Seal with heel of hand. Seal ends and fold sealed ends under. Place seam side down in greased pans. To make round loaf pull edges of dough under until ball is rounded and smooth. Place on a greased baking sheet round side up.

SECOND RISING

Cover bread pans or formed loaves with a cloth and let rise in a warm place (80 to 85°F.) until double in bulk. Dough in loaf pan should be well rounded with center above the pan. Test by pressing lightly with finger near edge of dough. If dent remains dough is ready to bake. Second rising takes about 45 minutes to 1 hour.

BAKING

Preheat oven to required temperature. Place pans on center shelf with 2 inches between them. If top browns too quickly, cover with foil. When bread is done, it will sound hollow when tapped lightly.

COOLING

As soon as breads are baked remove them from pans or baking sheets and place them on wire racks to cool.

PANS

Select correct pan sizes. A pan that is too large will result in bread that is not high enough. If pan is too small the dough will fall over the sides. Shiny bread pans need longer baking. For glass pans reduce temperature called for in recipe by 25°F.

RUTH'S JOURNEY BREAD

JOURNEY STARTER DOUGH

YEAST	granular, 1 tablespoon
WATER	warm, 2 cups
UNBLEACHED FLOUR	or all-purpose, 2 cups

In a 1 1/2 quart glass or earthenware container, mix the YEAST, WATER and FLOUR together. Leave in a warm place for 48 hours; stir several times. It will ferment, bubble and smell slightly sour. To use, stir, then spoon out as much starter as recipe requires. Add equal parts FLOUR and WATER to remaining starter in container. Stir and let stand about 4 hours or until it bubbles again before covering and refrigerating. By replenishing the starter with flour and water it can be used indefinitely in the Journey Bread Recipe.

JOURNEY BREAD

STARTER DOUGH	1 cup
WATER	warm, 1 cup
UNBLEACHED FLOUR	or all-purpose, 4 cups
HONEY	or sugar, 2 tablespoons
SALT	2 teaspoons

Put STARTER DOUGH in a large bowl and mix in WATER and 2 cups of FLOUR. Cover and let stand 24 hours in a warm place. Work in HONEY, SALT and enough FLOUR to make a dough that will clean the sides of the bowl and can be gathered into a ball. Turn dough out onto a lightly floured board and knead 10 minutes. Cover and let rest 15 minutes. Divide in half and shape into 2 round or oval loaves and place on a greased baking sheet. Make diagonal slashes on tops of loaves, cover and let rise in a warm place for 30 minutes. Bake in a preheated 375°F. oven about 35 minutes or until crust is golden brown.

NAOMI'S LITTLE BREADS

Journey Biscuits

WHOLE WHEAT FLOUR	1 1/4 cups
UNBLEACHED WHITE FLOUR	or all-purpose, 1 1/4 cups
BAKING POWDER	2 teaspoons
SALT	1/2 teaspoon
BUTTER	1/2 cup
STARTER DOUGH	2 cups
HONEY	or sugar, 2 tablespoons

Combine the two FLOURS, BAKING POWDER and SALT in a bowl. Cut in the BUTTER until the mixture resembles coarse meal. Mix in STARTER from preceding recipe and HONEY; beat well. Turn dough onto a lightly floured board and knead for 10 minutes. Roll out to 1/2 inch thickness; cut with a 2 1/2 inch cookie cutter. Place on a greased baking sheet 2 inches apart. Cover and let rise 1/2 hour in a warm place. Bake in a preheated 400°F. oven about 20 minutes or until lightly browned. If all WHITE FLOUR is used, reduce STARTER to 1 2/3 cups. Makes about 32 "biscuits."

Note: Commercial whole wheat flour is so refined and tasteless that it is better to get the whole wheat and grind it to the desired coarseness. Put not more than 1/4 cup at a time into a blender. Start on low speed; after 30 seconds, move the switch to high. Stop the blender occasionally so it does not overheat.

DAYBREAK BREAD

BARLEY FLOUR	1 1/2 cups
UNBLEACHED FLOUR	or all-purpose, 1/4 cup
BAKING POWDER	1 1/2 teaspoons
SALT	3/4 teaspoon
MILK	1 1/2 cups
EGG	1, beaten
OIL	2 tablespoons

Mix the first 4 ingredients together in a bowl. Add MILK and EGG stirring in well. Add OIL and mix only until blended; batter will look lumpy. Preheat a greased 9 inch square pan in a 450°F. oven for 2 to 3 minutes before pouring in the batter. Bake 20 to 25 minutes. Cut into strips and serve hot. Makes 18 strips 4 1/2 × 1 inches.

SOUR MILK AND BARLEY BREAD

YEAST	granular, 1 tablespoon
WATER	warm, 1/4 cup
SOUR MILK	1 cup at room temperature
OIL	1/4 cup

HONEY	1/4 cup
SALT	1 teaspoon
BARLEY FLOUR	2 cups
UNBLEACHED FLOUR	about 2 cups

Dissolve YEAST in warm WATER in a large bowl. Stir in the SOUR MILK, OIL, HONEY and SALT; mix well. Beat in the BARLEY FLOUR. Add enough of the UN-BLEACHED FLOUR to make a dough that will clean the sides of the bowl and can be gathered into a ball. Turn out onto a lightly floured board and knead 10 minutes. Place in a greased bowl, turning to grease top. Cover with a cloth and let rise in a warm place until double in bulk, about 1 1/2 hours. Punch down and let rise 1 hour. Shape into 2 round loaves about 5 inches in diameter. Place on a greased baking sheet. Cover and let rise 1 hour. Bake in a pre-heated 350°F. oven for 30 minutes or until bread sounds hollow when tapped. Remove to a rack to cool.
Note: To make sour milk, put 1 tablespoon vinegar into a cup. Fill cup with sweet milk. Let stand a few minutes.

BREAD WITH WHEY

YEAST	granular, 1 tablespoon
WHEY	(liquid from curd of cottage cheese —see cottage cheese recipe) or water, warm, 1 1/4 cups
OIL	3 tablespoons
SALT	1 teaspoon
HONEY	or sugar, 1 tablespoon
UNBLEACHED FLOUR	or all-purpose, 3 1/4 cups

Dissolve YEAST in WHEY. Add the next 3 ingredients and half the FLOUR. Beat well; mix in the remaining FLOUR. Dough will be sticky. Cover with a cloth and let rise in a warm place until double in bulk, about 1 hour. Stir down and beat about 30 strokes. Put dough into a well greased 9 × 5 × 3 inch loaf pan. Cover and let rise until dough reaches 1/4 inch from top of pan, about 45 minutes. Bake in a preheated 375°F. oven about 30 minutes or until golden brown and bread sounds hollow when tapped. Remove to a rack to cool. If WHEY is used the bread has a flavor of sourdough. Makes 1 loaf.

UNKNEADED BREAD OF THRACE

YEAST	granular, 1 tablespoon
WATER	1 1/4 cups, warm
OIL	2 tablespoons
SALT	1 teaspoon
HONEY	or sugar, 1 tablespoon
UNBLEACHED FLOUR	or all-purpose, 3 1/4 cups

Dissolve YEAST in WATER; add OIL, SALT, HONEY and half the FLOUR. Beat well and mix in remaining FLOUR. Cover with a cloth and let rise in a warm place until double in bulk, about 1 hour. Stir down batter and beat a few strokes. Turn into a well greased 9 × 5 × 3 inch loaf pan; with floured fingers pat dough smoothly into the pan. Cover and let rise 1 hour. Bake in a preheated 375°F. oven for 40 to 50 minutes or until loaf sounds hollow when tapped. Remove to a rack to cool. Makes 1 loaf.

HONEYED GRIDDLE CAKES

STARTER DOUGH	1 cup
WATER	warm, 2 cups
UNBLEACHED FLOUR	or all-purpose, 2 1/4 cups
EGGS	2, at room temperature
HONEY	or sugar, 2 tablespoons
OIL	2 tablespoons
MILK	1/3 cup
BAKING SODA	1 teaspoon
SALT	1/2 teaspoon

In a large bowl mix together the STARTER, WARM WATER and UNBLEACHED FLOUR. Cover and let stand overnight in a warm place free from drafts. Next morning, beat in the EGGS and the remaining ingredients; let stand 10 minutes. Drop batter onto a hot greased griddle making pancakes 4 to 5 inches in diameter. Flip cakes when surface bubbles form. Makes 4 1/2 cups of batter or about 20 five-inch griddle cakes. Serve with HONEY SYRUP.

PALESTINE FOUR FLOUR BREAD

YEAST	granular, 1 tablespoon
WATER	warm, 1 cup
EGG	1, at room temperature, beaten
OIL	3 tablespoons
HONEY	1/3 cup
ANISE SEED	ground, 1 teaspoon
NUTMEG	ground, 1 teaspoon
SALT	1 1/2 teaspoons
MILLET FLOUR	1/2 cup
LENTIL FLOUR	1/2 cup
BARLEY FLOUR	1/2 cup
UNBLEACHED WHITE FLOUR	2 to 2 1/2 cups

Dissolve YEAST in warm WATER. Stir in EGG, OIL, HONEY, ANISE, NUTMEG and SALT. Mix in the MILLET, LENTIL and BARLEY FLOUR and beat well. Add 2 cups of the UNBLEACHED FLOUR. Mix well and add enough more to make a dough that will clean the sides of the bowl and can be gathered into a ball. Turn out onto a lightly floured board and knead 10 minutes. Place in a greased bowl turning over to grease top surface. Cover with a cloth and let rise in a warm place until double in bulk, about 1 1/2 hours. Punch down and let rise again for 1 hour. Shape into 2 round loaves, about 5 inches in diameter, and place on a greased baking sheet. Cover and let rise 1 hour. Bake in a preheated 350°F. oven about 30 minutes or until bread sounds hollow when tapped. Remove to a rack to cool. Makes 2 loaves.
Note: See instructions for grinding millet, lentil, and barley under Naomi's Little Breads.

BREADS MANNA FROM HEAVEN

REBEKAH'S GRIDDLE BREADS

YEAST	granular, 1 tablespoon
WATER	warm, 1/2 cup
HONEY	2 teaspoons
SALT	1/2 teaspoon
MILK	warm, 1/2 cup
UNBLEACHED FLOUR	or all-purpose, 2 1/2 cups
BARLEY FLOUR	or coarse meal

Dissolve YEAST in WATER. Measure HONEY and SALT into a large bowl and stir in the MILK and dissolved YEAST. Add the FLOUR and mix well. Turn dough out onto a lightly floured board and knead until dough is smooth, about 5 minutes, using more flour if necessary. Cover with a cloth and let rest for 10 minutes. Sprinkle board with a light layer of BARLEY FLOUR and roll out dough to 1/2 inch in thickness. Sprinkle more BARLEY FLOUR lightly over the dough. Cut with a 3 inch floured cookie cutter. Place each round on a piece of waxed paper. Cover with a cloth and let rise in a warm place, until double in bulk. Heat a heavy ungreased griddle or skillet over low heat. Place as many rounds as possible on the griddle, without crowding. Cook very slowly, about 10 to 12 minutes on each side, turning once, until browned. Remove to a rack to cool. To serve, split and toast. Makes 10 Griddle Breads. Note: Barley flour is the hardest grain to grind and takes a longer time in the blender. Grind not more than 1/4 cup at a time, starting on low speed and switching to high, stopping occasionally so motor will not overheat.

SEED BREAD

UNBLEACHED FLOUR	3 cups
BAKING POWDER	4 teaspoons
SALT	1/2 teaspoon
BUTTER	1/3 cup
SUGAR	1 1/4 cups
EGGS	2
MILK	1 1/4 cups
ANISE SEED	1 tablespoon

Combine FLOUR, BAKING POWDER and SALT. In a medium bowl cream BUTTER and SUGAR; beat in EGGS one at a time. Alternately beat in flour mixture and MILK, one third at a time, until well mixed. Add ANISE SEED. Pour batter into a greased 9 × 5 × 3 inch loaf pan and bake about 1 hour in a preheated 350°F. oven or until a cake tester inserted in the center comes out clean. Cool on a rack 10 minutes; remove from pan; finish cooling. Makes 1 loaf.

EZEKIEL'S MANY-FLOURED BREAD

YEAST	granular, 2 tablespoons
WATER	warm, 1 1/2 cups
EGG	1, at room temperature
OIL	5 tablespoons, reserve 1 tablespoon to brush top of breads
HONEY	1/3 cup
SALT	2 1/2 teaspoons
CUMIN SEED	ground, 1 tablespoon
CORIANDER SEED	ground, 1 tablespoon
LENTIL FLOUR	1/4 cup red or brown
BARLEY FLOUR	1/4 cup
FAVA or BROAD BEAN FLOUR	1/4 cup
MILLET FLOUR	1/4 cup
WHOLE WHEAT FLOUR	2 cups
UNBLEACHED WHITE FLOUR	1 to 2 1/2 cups

Dissolve YEAST in warm WATER. Mix in the next six ingredients. Stir in all the flours, with the exception of the UNBLEACHED WHITE FLOUR and beat well. Add enough of the UNBLEACHED FLOUR to make a dough that will clean the sides of the bowl and can be gathered into a ball. Turn out onto a lightly floured board and knead 10 minutes. Place in a greased bowl, turning over to grease top surface. Cover with a cloth and let rise in a warm place until double in bulk, about 1 1/2 hours. Punch down and let rise again about 1 hour. Shape into 2 round loaves and place on a greased baking sheet or in 2 greased 8 1/2 ×

4 1/2 × 2 5/8 inch loaf pans. Cover and let rise 1 hour. Bake in a preheated 350°F. oven for about 30 minutes or until bread sounds hollow when tapped. Remove to a rack to cool and brush with remaining tablespoon of OIL. Makes 2 loaves.

Note: See instructions for grinding lentils, barley, fava beans, millet and whole wheat under Naomi's Little Breads.

SINAI HERB BREAD

YEAST	granular, 2 tablespoons
WATER	warm, 1/4 cup
HONEY	1/4 cup
BUTTER	1/4 cup, melted
SALT	1 teaspoon
MILK	1 cup, warm
EGGS	2, at room temperature, slightly beaten
DILL WEED	2 teaspoons chopped fresh or 1 teaspoon dried
MARJORAM	2 teaspoons chopped fresh or 1 teaspoon dried
TARRAGON	2 teaspoons chopped fresh or 1 teaspoon dried
NUTMEG	ground, 1/4 teaspoon
UNBLEACHED FLOUR	4 1/2 to 5 cups

Dissolve YEAST in WATER. Mix in the remaining ingredients with the exception of the FLOUR. Add 3 cups FLOUR and beat well. Add enough of the remaining FLOUR to make a dough that will clean the sides of the bowl and can be gathered into a ball. Turn out onto a lightly floured board and knead 10 minutes. Place in a greased bowl, turning over to grease top surface. Cover with a cloth and let rise in a warm place until double in bulk, about 1 hour. Punch down, divide in half and shape into 2 round loaves or place into 2 greased 8 1/2 × 4 1/2 × 2 5/8 inch bread pans. Cover and let rise again until double in bulk, about 1 hour. Bake in a preheated 375°F. oven for 20 to 30 minutes or until loaves sound hollow when tapped. Remove to a rack to cool. Makes 2 loaves.

bReaDS MANNA fROM heaven

SPICED BREAD GALATIA

YEAST	granular, 1 tablespoon
WATER	warm, 1/4 cup
EGG	1 at room temperature, beaten
MILK	warm, 3/4 cup
OIL	1/4 cup
HONEY	3 tablespoons
CORIANDER SEED	ground, 1 tablespoon
CUMIN SEED	ground, 1/2 teaspoon
CINNAMON	ground, 1/4 teaspoon
SALT	1 teaspoon
WHOLE WHEAT FLOUR	2 cups
UNBLEACHED FLOUR	1 to 1 1/2 cups

Dissolve YEAST in warm WATER in a large bowl. Stir in EGG, MILK, OIL, HONEY, SPICES and SALT; stir in WHOLE WHEAT FLOUR and beat well. Add enough UN-BLEACHED FLOUR to make a dough that will clean the sides of the bowl and can be gathered into a ball. Turn out onto a lightly floured board and knead 10 minutes. Place in a greased bowl, turning to grease top. Cover with a cloth and let rise in a warm place until double in bulk, 1 1/2 hours. Punch down and shape into a round loaf about 7 inches in diameter. Place on a greased baking sheet; cover and let rise 1 hour. Bake in a preheated 350°F. oven for 30 minutes or until bread sounds hollow when tapped. Remove to a rack to cool. Makes 1 loaf.

THESSALONICA ONION BREAD

WATER	warm, 1 cup
YEAST	granular, 1 tablespoon
HONEY	or sugar, 2 teaspoons
SALT	1 1/2 teaspoons
OIL	1/4 cup
UNBLEACHED FLOUR	or all purpose, 2 1/2 to 3 cups
ONIONS	1 cup, chopped

Sprinkle YEAST over WATER, let stand 2 to 3 minutes and

stir to dissolve. Add HONEY, 1 teaspoon SALT, 2 tablespoons OIL and 2 cups FLOUR; beat until well blended. Add enough additional FLOUR to make a dough that will clean the sides of the bowl and can be gathered into a ball. Turn out onto a lightly floured board and knead 10 minutes. Place in greased bowl, turning over once to grease top surface. Cover with a cloth and let rise in a warm place until double in bulk, about 1 hour. Punch down and divide in half. Put dough into 2 greased 8 inch round cake pans. Divide uncooked ONIONS and press lightly into dough covering entire top surface. Let rise in a warm place, uncovered, until double in bulk, about 1 hour. Brush with remaining 2 tablespoons OIL and sprinkle with 1/2 teaspoon SALT. Bake in a preheated 375°F. oven about 25 minutes or until bread sounds hollow when tapped. Remove from pans and cool on a wire rack. Serve warm. Makes 2 loaves.

LEAVENED BREAD

YEAST	granular, 1 tablespoon
WATER	2 cups, lukewarm
SALT	2 teaspoons
OLIVE OIL	2 tablespoons
HONEY	1 tablespoon
UNBLEACHED FLOUR	or whole wheat, 5 to 6 cups

Sprinkle YEAST over lukewarm WATER; let stand 2 to 3 minutes and stir to dissolve. Stir in SALT, OLIVE OIL and HONEY. Beat in 3 1/2 cups of FLOUR and add enough remaining FLOUR to form a dough that can be gathered into a ball. Place on a lightly floured board and knead 10 minutes. Place in a greased bowl, turning over to grease the top surface. Cover with a cloth and let rise in a warm place until dough is double in bulk, about 1 hour. Punch down, form into a ball and cut into 8 equal pieces. Roll out each one to 1/4 inch thickness, about 6 inches in diameter. Place on a baking sheet, cover and let rise 45 minutes. Bake in a preheated 500°F. oven for 10 to 12 minutes or until golden. If oven has cooled due to opening door, return to 500°F.

before putting in the next batch. Remove from oven and wrap in a towel until ready to serve. The loaves will be puffed and have a pocket of air in the center. Makes 8 loaves.

DAVID'S RESCUE
Leavened Shewbread

YEAST	granular, 2 tablespoons
WATER	1/2 cup, warm
BUTTER	3 tablespoons, soft
HONEY	3 tablespoons, or sugar
SALT	2 teaspoons
MILK	1 1/4 cups, warm
BUCKWHEAT GROATS	or cracked wheat, 1/2 cup
UNBLEACHED FLOUR	or all-purpose, 4 to 5 cups
OIL	

Dissolve YEAST in warm WATER; mix in the next 4 ingredients. Stir in the BUCKWHEAT GROATS and 2 cups of the UNBLEACHED FLOUR and beat well. Add enough of the remaining FLOUR to make a dough that will clean the sides of the bowl and can be gathered into a ball. Place in a greased bowl, turning over to grease the top. Cover with a cloth and let rise in a warm place until double in bulk, about 1 hour. Punch down and turn out onto a lightly floured board. Cover with a cloth and let rise on the board for 15 minutes. Form into a ball and divide in half. Divide each half into 6 wedges and form each into a ball. Place on 2 greased baking sheets. Press flat to make a loaf about 3 1/2 inches in diameter; space 3 inches apart. Brush tops with OIL. Cover and let rise 1 hour. Bake in a preheated 375°F. oven about 20 minutes or until golden. Remove from oven and brush tops again with OIL; place on wire racks. Serve warm with butter. Makes 12 shewbreads.

GOLAN DISCS
Unleavened Bread

UNBLEACHED FLOUR	4 cups
SALT	1 teaspoon
WATER	1 1/2 cups, at room temperature

Combine the FLOUR and SALT. Add enough WATER to make a dough that will clean the sides of the bowl and can be gathered into a ball. Turn out onto a lightly floured board and knead 10 minutes. Shape into a ball and cut in half. Cut each half into 8 pieces and form into 16 balls. Roll out each ball to form about a 7 inch circle. Place on an ungreased baking sheet and bake in a preheated 500°F. oven for 5 minutes or until discs are lightly colored, blistered and crisp. Serve with cheese, dips, and soups. Makes 16 discs.

CAESAREA THINS
Unleavened Shewbread

WATER	warm, 1 1/2 cups
OIL	3 tablespoons
HONEY	3 tablespoons
SALT	1 tablespoon
BUCKWHEAT GROATS	1/4 cup
UNBLEACHED FLOUR	or all-purpose, 3 3/4 to 4 cups

In a bowl mix the first 5 ingredients together. Add half of the UNBLEACHED FLOUR and beat well. Mix in enough of the remaining FLOUR to make a dough that will clean the sides of the bowl and can be gathered into a ball. Turn out onto a lightly floured board and knead 10 minutes. Shape into a ball and cut in half; cut each half into 6 equal pieces. Form the 12 pieces into balls and roll each out to 1/16 inch thickness. Cut with a 1 3/4 inch cookie cutter. Roll each circle again to measure about 3 inches in diameter; they must be very thin. Place on an ungreased baking sheet in a preheated 375°F. oven for 3 to 5 minutes or until the edges are brown. Serve with cheese, dips and soup. Makes about 12 dozen.

HERDSMAN'S CAKE

UNBLEACHED FLOUR	2 1/3 cups
BAKING POWDER	1 1/2 teaspoons
NUTMEG	1/4 teaspoon
CARAWAY SEEDS	2 teaspoons
BUTTER	2/3 cup
DATE SUGAR	or brown, 2/3 cup
EGGS	2
MILK	2/3 cup

Combine the first 4 ingredients in a bowl and cut in BUTTER until mixture resembles coarse meal; mix in DATE SUGAR. Beat EGGS and MILK together in a small bowl; stir into flour mixture; do not beat. Pour into a greased 8 1/2 × 4 1/2 × 2 5/8 inch pan. Bake in a preheated 350°F. oven about 50 minutes or until cake tester comes out clean. Remove to a cake rack and serve slightly warm, cut into thin slices. Serve with a soft cheese.

APRICOT NUT BREAD

APRICOTS	dried, 1/2 cup
SUGAR	3/4 cup
BAKING POWDER	5 teaspoons
BAKING SODA	1/2 teaspoon
SALT	1/2 teaspoon
UNBLEACHED FLOUR	2 1/4 cups
EGG	1, well beaten
BUTTERMILK	1 cup
OIL	1 tablespoon
PISTACHIO NUTS	or walnuts, 1 cup, chopped

Cut APRICOTS into thin slivers. Combine the next 5 ingredients reserving 2 tablespoons of FLOUR to dredge APRICOTS and NUTS. Mix the EGG with BUTTERMILK and OIL and add to dry ingredients, stirring only until mixed. Fold in the dredged APRICOTS and NUTS. Spoon into a greased 9 × 5 × 3 inch loaf pan. Bake in a preheated 350°F. oven for about an hour or until a cake tester inserted in the center comes out clean. Turn out onto a rack to cool. Makes 1 loaf.

Note: This bread slices better the second day.

"LITTLE ARMS" PRETZELS

WATER	1 1/2 cups, warm
YEAST	1 tablespoon
SUGAR	1/4 cup
UNBLEACHED FLOUR	4 1/2 cups
EGG	1, beaten with 2 teaspoons water
SALT	coarse

Stir together WATER, YEAST and SUGAR in a large bowl. Let stand 1 hour. Mix in FLOUR thoroughly. Turn dough out on lightly floured surface and knead 10 minutes. Grease bowl, return dough to bowl, turning to grease the top. Cover and set in a warm place to rise until double in size, about 1 1/2 hours. Punch down, then pinch off a piece of dough about the size of a golf ball. Roll dough with hands to 15 inches long or pull into a smooth rope. Make a loop by picking up and crossing the ends of the rolled strips. Bring the left end of the strip over to the right and then the right end over to the left. This forms a twist in the center. Bring the ends up and over and press them against the sides of the loop, making the traditional pretzel shape. Place the pretzels on greased cookie sheets two inches apart. In a small bowl, beat EGG with water and brush on each one. Sprinkle with coarse SALT. Let dough rise again, 1/2 to 3/4 hour. Bake in a preheated 475°F. oven 10 to 12 minutes until golden. Cool on rack. Makes about 2 dozen.

Note: These pretzels can also be made in stick form.

BREADS MANNA FROM HEAVEN

TEA BREAD PHENICE

UNBLEACHED FLOUR	or all-purpose, 1 cup
WHOLE WHEAT FLOUR	1 cup
BAKING POWDER	1 teaspoon
BAKING SODA	1 teaspoon
SALT	1/8 teaspoon
EGG	1
BUTTERMILK	3/4 cup
SOUR CREAM	1/4 cup
GRENADINE SYRUP	or maple, 3/4 cup

Combine the first 5 ingredients. Mix the EGG and the remaining ingredients together. Stir the liquid ingredients slowly into the dry and mix well. Pour into a greased 8 1/2 × 4 1/2 × 2 5/8 inch cake pan and bake in a preheated 325°F. oven for about 1 hour or until cake tester comes out clean. Let cool in pan 10 minutes before removing to a rack.

DATE NUT BREAD

WATER	warm, 1/4 cup
YEAST	granular, 1 tablespoon
MILK	warm, 1 cup
HONEY	or sugar, 1 tablespoon
SALT	1 teaspoon
CINNAMON	1 teaspoon, ground
OIL	2 tablespoons
WHOLE WHEAT FLOUR	1/2 cup
UNBLEACHED FLOUR	2 to 2 1/2 cups
DATES	or raisins, 1/2 cup, chopped
PINE NUTS	or walnuts, 1/2 cup, coarsely chopped

Sprinkle YEAST over WATER; let stand 2 to 3 minutes and stir until dissolved. Add MILK, HONEY, SALT, CINNAMON and 1 1/2 tablespoons OIL. Stir in WHOLE WHEAT FLOUR and 1 cup of the UNBLEACHED FLOUR and beat well. Add DATES and NUTS and enough additional UNBLEACHED FLOUR to make a dough that will clean the sides of the bowl and can be gathered into a ball. Turn out onto a lightly floured board and knead 10 minutes. Cover dough on board with a cloth and let rest 20 minutes; punch dough down and divide in half. Form into 2 loaves and place in 2 greased 7 3/8 × 3 5/8 × 2 1/4 inch loaf pans. Cover with a cloth and let rise in a warm place until double in bulk or until dough reaches the top of the pan. Bake in a preheated 375°F. oven for about 25 to 30 minutes or until bread sounds hollow when tapped. Brush with remaining OIL and remove to a rack to cool. Makes 2 loaves.

BUTTERMILK PANCAKES

WHOLE WHEAT FLOUR	1 cup
BAKING POWDER	1 teaspoon
BAKING SODA	1/2 teaspoon
SALT	1 teaspoon
SUGAR	1 teaspoon
EGGS	2, separated
OIL	2 tablespoons
BUTTERMILK	2 cups

Combine the first 5 ingredients in a bowl. Beat the EGG yolks, add the OIL and BUTTERMILK; combine with the dry ingredients. Beat the EGG whites until stiff and fold in. Drop the batter by tablespoonfuls onto a hot greased griddle; when they are golden on one side, turn. Serve with honey. Makes about 30 pancakes.

SOUR CREAM PANCAKES

UNBLEACHED FLOUR	or all-purpose, 1/2 cup
BAKING POWDER	1/2 teaspoon
SUGAR	1 teaspoon
ANISE SEED	1 teaspoon
SALT	1/2 teaspoon
EGGS	2, beaten
SOUR CREAM	1/2 cup
CREAMED COTTAGE CHEESE	1/2 cup

Mix the dry ingredients together; add the beaten EGGS

and stir in the SOUR CREAM and COTTAGE CHEESE. Cook on a hot greased griddle or skillet, turning once after bubbles form. Serve with HONEY SYRUP Makes about 16 three inch pancakes.

HONEY SYRUP

WATER 1 cup
SUGAR 1 cup
HONEY 1/4 cup

Bring WATER, SUGAR and HONEY to a boil and simmer over low heat 30 minutes. Cool. Makes 1 1/4 cups.

BETHLEHEM BARLEY AND ONIONS

BARLEY 1 cup
BUTTER 3 tablespoons
ONIONS 1 cup, finely chopped
STOCK beef, 3 cups
SALT
PEPPER

Heat BARLEY in a dry skillet until it becomes lightly colored and has a nutty fragrance. Add the next 3 ingredients. Cover tightly and simmer 50 to 60 minutes or until liquid is absorbed and BARLEY is tender. SALT and PEPPER to taste. Serve with lamb or fowl. Serves 6 to 8

FIRMITY

Joseph's Gift To Benjamin

BUCKWHEAT GROATS	or kasha, 1 cup
MILK	2 cups
SALT	1 teaspoon
GREEN ONIONS	1/2 cup, chopped
HONEY	1/4 cup
BUTTER	3 tablespoons

Combine BUCKWHEAT GROATS and MILK in a saucepan; add the next 3 ingredients. Cover tightly and cook 20 minutes over low heat. Stir several times during the cooking to keep from sticking. Remove the cover and cook 5 minutes more. Stir in BUTTER; correct the seasoning. Serve with meat. Serves 4 to 6.

Note: Firmity was a dish of hulled wheat boiled in milk and reputed to have been sent by Joseph to Benjamin.

TARSUS PIE
Millet With Cheese Sauce

WATER	4 1/2 cups
SALT	1 1/2 teaspoons
NUTMEG	freshly grated, 1/8 teaspoon
MILLET	1 1/2 cups, ground
SAUCE FOR SAUL	

Bring WATER to a boil and stir in SALT, NUTMEG and the MILLET gradually so the WATER does not stop boiling. Reduce heat and continue cooking, uncovered, stirring occasionally until the MILLET is very thick, about 1 hour. Pour into a well greased 9 inch pie plate; cool and refrigerate until firm. Prepare sauce.

SAUCE FOR SAUL

BUTTER	3 tablespoons
FLOUR	3 1/2 tablespoons
MILK	1 1/2 cups
SALT	1/4 teaspoon
ROMANO CHEESE	grated, 1/2 cup

Melt BUTTER in saucepan. Stir in FLOUR and cook for 1 minute. Add MILK slowly and stir until smooth and thickened. Add SALT; reserve. Turn the MILLET out onto a flat surface and split in half horizontally. Return bottom half to pie plate and spread over one half the SAUCE FOR SAUL. Replace top half and pour over the remaining sauce. Sprinkle with grated ROMANO CHEESE and bake for 20 minutes in a 400°F. oven. Put under the broiler a few seconds until golden. Serves 4 to 6.

MILLET JUDEA

Millet With Nuts And Raisins

MILLET	1 cup
CHICKEN STOCK	3 cups
ONION	1 cup, chopped
BUTTER	1/4 cup
SALT	1 teaspoon
GOLDEN RAISINS	1/4 cup
PISTACHIO NUTS	or almonds, toasted and slivered, 1/4 cup

Toast MILLET in an ungreased skillet over medium heat, stirring constantly, for 3 or 4 minutes or until golden. Add remaining ingredients except the nuts. Tightly cover and simmer over low heat for 15 minutes or until MILLET is tender and STOCK is absorbed. Stir in NUTS and toss lightly. Correct seasoning. Serve with game or poultry. Serves 6.

"CORN"

ONIONS	1 cup, chopped
BUTTER	6 tablespoons
LENTILS	1/4 cup
BARLEY	1/4 cup
MILLET	1/4 cup
CRACKED WHEAT	1/4 cup
CUMIN SEED	1/4 teaspoon, ground
SALT	3/4 teaspoon
WATER	2 cups

In a medium-sized saucepan, cook the ONIONS in BUTTER until golden; add the remaining ingredients. Cover with a tight fitting lid and cook over low heat for 20 minutes; remove the cover and cook 5 minutes more. Stir several times during the cooking to prevent sticking. The WATER should be absorbed and the grain tender. Serve with meat or fowl with or without gravy. Serves 4 to 6.
Note: "Corn" in biblical times meant a mixture of lentils, barley, millet, wheat and cumin.

ABRAM'S SUPPER
Cracked Wheat And Bacon

CRACKED WHEAT	1 cup
BACON	8 slices, cut into 1/2 inch pieces
ONION	1 1/2 cups, chopped
WATER	2 cups
SALT	1/2 teaspoon
BUTTER	2 tablespoons
EGGS	2, hard-cooked, chopped
PARSLEY	2 tablespoons, chopped

Toast CRACKED WHEAT in a dry saucepan over low heat, shaking pan and stirring to prevent burning, for 5 to 8 minutes. In a skillet cook BACON pieces until crisp; remove and drain on a paper towel. Cook ONIONS until golden in the BACON fat. Add the ONIONS and fat to the toasted CRACKED WHEAT; stir in WATER and SALT. Cover tightly and cook 20 minutes. Stir several times during the cooking to keep from sticking. Remove cover and cook 5 minutes more. Stir in BUTTER and chopped EGGS; toss well and correct seasoning. Sprinkle with PARSLEY and BACON. Serve with cold meats and a salad. Serves 4 to 6.